READ MY LIFE AND TRAVEL EXPERIENCES AND I WILL THROW IN A KID

JUDY TARVIN

ISBN 979-8-88644-346-2 (Paperback)
ISBN 979-8-88644-348-6 (Hardcover)
ISBN 979-8-88644-347-9 (Digital)

All biblical citations were taken from the King James
Version of the Holy Bible unless otherwise indicated.

Covenant Books
11661 Hwy 707
Murrells Inlet, SC 29576
www.covenantbooks.com

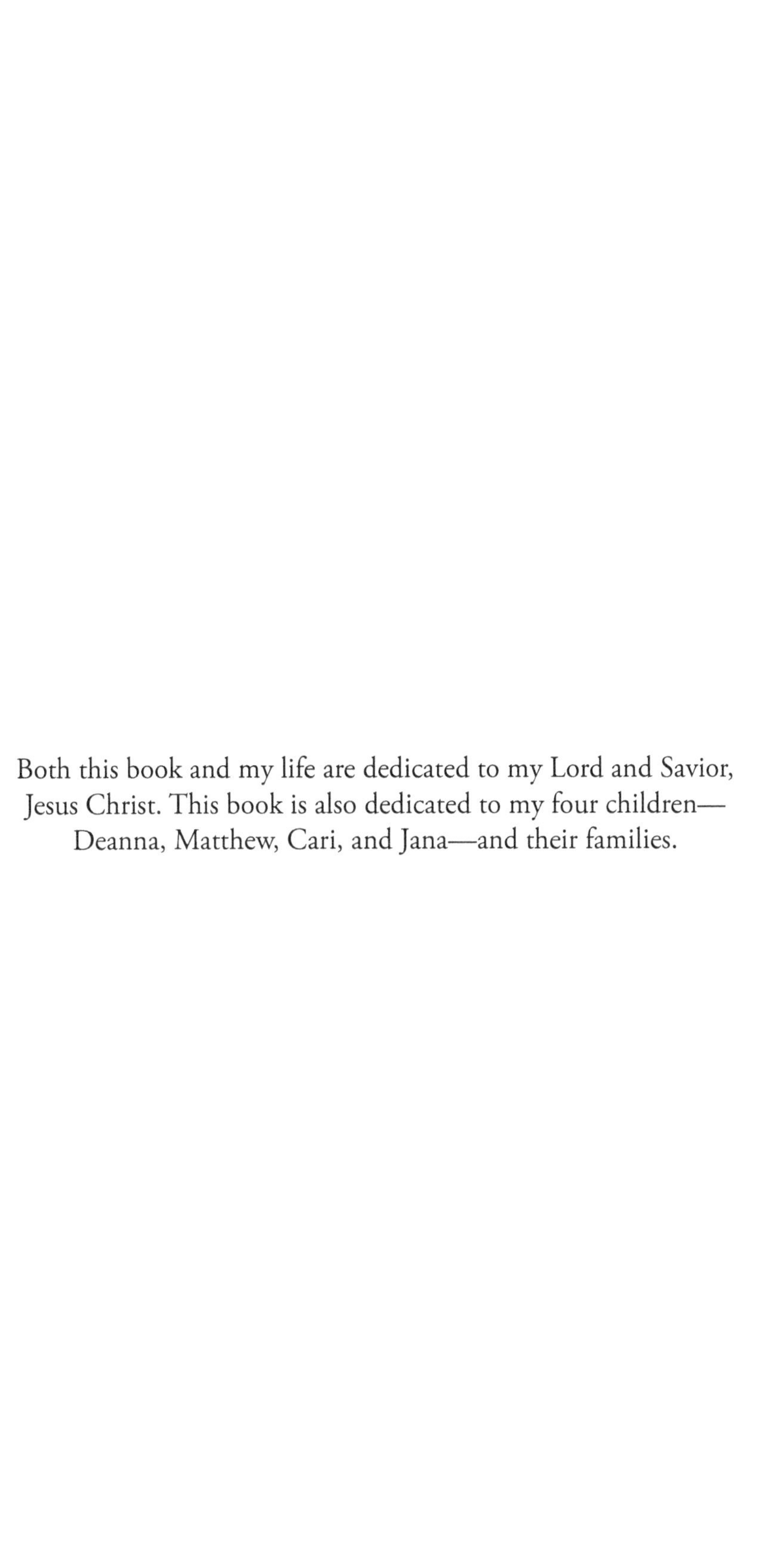

Both this book and my life are dedicated to my Lord and Savior, Jesus Christ. This book is also dedicated to my four children— Deanna, Matthew, Cari, and Jana—and their families.

⟨∘⟨⟩∘⟩

PREFACE

All the stories you will read in this book are true. My life and travel experiences are a collection of true short stories—mostly funny, some serious, some informational to the location, and some spiritual, covering over seventy years. I will share personal insights on the road to my relationship with Jesus Christ in hopes that you, too, will not only know of him but will truly know him. My most favorite verse among the hundreds in the Bible, which has guided me through many things:

> Call unto me, and I will answer thee, and
> show thee great and mighty things, which thou
> knowest not. (Jeremiah 33:3)

Let me explain the "kid" part of this book. My oldest child was six years old when I became a believer, and it could not have come at a better time. Her daddy was lost to the war in Vietnam, so I was a single mom for a while. Then later, a son came along and, even later, two daughters. There is no way I could have raised these kids without the help of Jesus growing me so I could grow them. The things I learned along the way from the Bible were paramount in my life and theirs. However, there were many laughs along the way and many times when I just had to shake my head and go on. I am sure you will relate.

Life is like a beautiful bowl of cherries,
Throw out the pits, and you have the
Sweet fruit of the vine.

Jesus said in John 15:1,
"I AM the true vine,
And my Father is the husbandman."

LIFE EXPERIENCES

Life is full of experiences, but often we do not remember those experiences because we do not take the opportunity to share them. When we tell our stories to others, it also imprints them on our minds to help us remember the good times. Remembering helps us keep track of how God has answered our prayers and how God has shown us a better way or brought an experience into our lives that helps make us a better person. It reminds us how God has brought different people into the forefront of our living. We have experiences with our parents, stepparents, siblings, twelve years of school friends, teachers, college classmates, career or business coworkers, church friends, and those we meet in our travels. There are lots of stories to be told. Here are some more of mine.

I covered many stories in my first book, *Read My Life and Travel Experiences and I Will Throw in a Cake.* Now I am going to add more life stories, travel stories, and include some of the stories from the raising of my kids, and the enjoyment of my grandkids.

When you are a child, you act like a child

My mother told me this story many times. We were living in Los Angeles, and she took me and my brother to the post office with her. While standing in line, a lady spoke kindly to me, and while she was telling me how cute I was, I got shy, picked up the hem of my dress, and put it in my mouth. Now that would have been a sweet experience with a four-year-old, except for one thing, I did not have any underwear on. Then, as though that was not shock enough for my mother, as we walked down the street, my two-year-old brother saw a bearded man and yelled out, "Mama, there's Jesus!"

Almost lost forever

I was about two years old, shopping with my mother in a department store, and while she was paying for her purchases, an older lady walked by, took my hand, and started out the door with me. I went without so much as a word as she walked me out the department store door. My mother came screaming after me, and the woman let go of my hand and disappeared. I could have been kidnapped and forever lived a quite different life. I am quite sure there was a guardian angel watching me because God knew my future.

> For he shall give his angels charge over thee,
> to keep thee in all thy ways. (Psalm 91:11)

> Before I formed thee in the belly I knew
> thee; and before thou camest forth out of the
> womb I sanctified thee, and I ordained thee a
> prophet unto the nations. (Jeremiah 1:5)

I believe that God knows every person born like he did Jeremiah and has a plan for their lives.

The Grand Canyon deer

When I was about six, our family was traveling to visit the Grand Canyon. We stopped at picnic tables along the highway to eat lunches our mother packed. On one of those days, several deer came out of the woods to join us. They were not shy and were hoping for a handout. One of them took a piece of bread right out of my hand.

I loved that experience, and today, I enjoy feeding the deer in my backyard every winter. Last year, I counted eighteen does in my yard at one time.

Lizard makes a U-turn

Another stop along the way, we were encouraged to run around in a dried-up riverbed. However, it was not fun for my brother. A lizard had found its way up my brother's pant leg. He started screaming and danced around like a madman. The lizard must have then made a U-turn and proceeded down the other pant leg and out, which caused my brother to continue screaming and dancing. I never thought to ask him how that impacted his childhood.

Snakeskin is still scary

While my father was working a summer job at Boulder Dam in Nevada, we lived there at the base of a mountain. It was like a camp for the families of those who were working for the dam. My brother and I had a few frightful experiences while we were there. We were playing on the side of the mountain when we came across a huge, long snake. We ran all the way home, and my dad went looking for it, only to discover that it was nothing more than the skin a large snake had shed.

Tarantulas are equally scary

At the same camp, we walked with our mother to the office, and on the counter in a large glass bowl was a live tarantula. It scared me. I hate spiders! I backed up, and the clerk reached into the bowl, took the tarantula out of the bowl, and asked me if I wanted to hold it. I told her emphatically, "No." She said they do not bite, but I did not care, and my mother had a few words for that clerk.

I hate snakes

That area was known for rattlesnakes, and we saw a few. I was sitting on a blanket in the front yard with my brother and, suddenly, my mother yelled at us to get up and run to her quickly. We obeyed immediately. She saw the snake on its way toward our blanket. Our dad killed it.

Potatoes and bullheads

One year, our mom and her friends rented a cabin along the Idaho river on a property that was growing potatoes. They fished for bullheads and had outdoor fish fries. I remember what looked like laundry tubs filled with fish. They sang and danced, but my brother and I played in the potato fields and the irrigation ditches. We washed little potatoes in the ditches and ate them raw. We also took part in the owner's fall festival. His house was at the top of a hill, and the road sparkled with lights all the way up. There were lots of tasty food and games, music, and dancing. It was magical.

Aboard the USS Saint Paul

We lived in Torrance, California, for a year or so before our family moved to the Midwest. That is where our mother met our stepfather. He was a marine and was onboard the USS *Saint Paul* and was sent to Korea. We watched the news every night to make sure the ship he was on was safe. What we did not know was that the marines were put off the ship and were engaged in the boots on the ground war. My stepdad came home safe, but we lost between 35,000 and 40,000 American men in just three years. What a sad outcome.

Who chews tar?

The fog was dense in California, but my brother and I loved to play hide and seek with neighbor kids. Also, we would all spend time watching the road crews spread tar on the roads. Sometimes, we would chew a piece of tar like gum. It sounds gross to me now, but that is what we did.

Goodbye, sunny California

Our life takes a turn in 1950 when our parents divorced. Our mother married our stepdad, Merle, and moved us to the Midwest. Our dad married our stepmom, Charlene, and they moved to Oregon. It was goodbye, sunny California. No more sandy beaches, no more giant pretzels, no more orange groves, Disneyland, Knotts Berry Farm, or San Diego Zoo. That is a lot for a kid to give up for snow, ice, and farmland.

Traveling with goldfish and a dog

Our trip to the Midwest was interesting. Our car was small, but there were two adults, three kids, one dog, and a bowl of goldfish. The goldfish were on the floor in the front seat, between my mother's feet. The dog was in the back seat with the three of us kids, ages nine, seven, and two. When lunchtime came around, mother made us sandwiches from the front seat and handed them to us in the back seat. Sometimes, our sandwiches accidentally hit the floor for the dog. Our belongings went ahead to Hastings, Nebraska, where our stepdad finished his tour of duty at the marine base there.

Peg leg

Hastings was a fun place for kids. There were cobblestone streets downtown. We walked to our swimming lessons and got ice cream on the way home. We lived in a large house on a big corner lot. Our stepdad raked up leaves for us to jump in. At least that is what we thought he did it for. In the winter, he also played a game of fencing with us using long icicles. There was a train that passed by up on the hill, behind our house every day. One day, our dog was hit by the train. It broke his leg, so he had a cast on one front leg. We called him peg leg and laughed every time we heard him coming.

Bathtub full of laundry

I got into a bit of trouble, one day, trying to do a good deed. My mother was about to have my second baby brother, and she was tired all the time. I decided that I would help her out by doing the laundry. Sounds like a wonderful thing to do, except that we had no washer or dryer yet. My mother or my stepdad took our laundry to the laundromat, but of course, I could not do that. So I gathered clothes, filled the bathtub with hot water and soap, and was washing the clothes and wringing them out by hand when my mother came in.

She was not as happy as I had hoped. I do not remember the outcome of that, but I do know as a mother myself in that situation, I would not have been happy about a bathtub full of wet laundry that had to go to the laundromat. Someone would have had to wring out every garment by hand and transport it to the laundromat for proper washing and drying.

Homemade bread

My mother learned how to bake homemade bread, and she did an excellent job of providing hot bread every week. Most of the time, we had margarine on the table, but when the bread came out of the oven, she spread it with real butter. What a treat that was and still is. I was just remembering that we bought margarine in a bag. It was white and there was a bit of orange coloring in the bag that we would squeeze and squeeze until the entire bag was yellow. As a mom baking bread for my family, I would reserve one loaf right out of the oven, spread with butter to be gobbled down with gusto.

Marines do not wear lace and bows

My stepdad played baseball with the marine's team. We went to all the games. My mother was a bit of a prankster and, one week, she sewed lace and pink bows on my stepdad's uniform. She packed up his bag for him and made sure he was just going to make it in time to hit the locker room. He pulled out his uniform and had no choice but to put it on.

After the game was over, my stepdad's commanding officer came up to my mother with an angry look on his face and said, "Jan, are you up for sewing lace and bows on all the marine's uniforms?"

Such drama

I got into a fight after school one day in the fifth grade. I do not remember why, but one girl told me to meet her in the gym after school. She brought two other girls with her, and she beat me up. She only punched me a couple of times and sat on me, but I was not hurt. It may have had something to do with the fact that we were all in Girl Scouts together, and I drew the winning number that made me the princess of the Girl Scout Ball. Oh, such drama, but I went to the ball in a beautiful dress my mother made for me and a crown on my head.

Here comes Santa Claus

My parents were having a tough time financially while we lived in Hastings. My mother did not work, my dad sent child support, but it was not very much. My stepdad was a corporal in the marine corps, and that was all their income for a while. But there were three things that made me happy while we lived there. First, my mother made homemade bread every week. Second, my stepdad would bring home leftover platters of meats and cheeses from the base chow hall. Thirdly, on Christmas Eve, Santa Claus would go up and down the streets at night with his reindeer sleigh. My brother and I would press our noses against the window, watching and waiting. We saw him every year that we lived there.

Farm life is not for me

I must tell you that I found out, by the age of ten, that farm life was not for me. When my stepdad's tour with the marine corps was over, we moved to Sioux City, Iowa, for a time while my stepdad attended barber school. While we were there, we visited his parents and siblings who lived on a farm in Bronson, Iowa. My stepdad was the oldest in his family. He had one sister and two brothers. His brothers were closest to our age, and they felt more like cousins than uncles. They were Larry and Jerry. Here are four stories from my first book regarding the farm life that was not for me.

The outhouse

I voiced my disdain for the outhouse to Jerry, and we decided we would improve the potty process. I do not remember how we got the paint, but we found part of a can of pink and part of a can of blue. We proceeded to paint one side pink for the girls and the other side blue for the boys. We even drew up signs to indicate the above so there would be no doubt as to which side you belonged in. We also supplied each side with more toilet paper and paper dinner napkins as well. We got rid of the Sears and Montgomery Ward catalogs. Well, that did not go over well with the adults in the house. My stepdad's father made us repaint it all gray and bought us new paint brushes.

Milk straight from the cow

The boys milked the cows by hand and brought it directly into the house, to the refrigerator. My grandma filled five-gallon milk jugs and allowed the cream to rise to the top. My problem was the smell.

To me, the milk tasted like how the barn smelled. I detected it in my cereal and anything my grandma cooked or baked that had milk in it.

Chicken? Not for me, thanks!

Then there were the Sunday dinners that were always fried chicken. My grandpa invited me out into the yard to watch him catch a chicken for dinner. I sat on the steps while he and Jerry chased a few chickens until one was caught. There was a tree stump close to the steps, and they headed for it with the chicken in hand. As I innocently watched, grandpa held the body of the chicken, and Jerry stretched its neck across the stump. Suddenly, my grandpa had a hatchet which came down on the chicken's neck. Blood spurted everywhere as the chicken was released, and it ran around the yard without its head. As a ten-year-old city girl, I was traumatized. My grandma scolded my grandpa and took me in the house. Later, grandpa came and said he was sorry, but there was no getting me to eat chicken for dinner.

Cow pies are not stepping-stones

One Sunday after church, Jerry and I were to pick apples in the orchard along the side of the cow pasture. I noticed the large cow pies along the muddy trail. I asked Jerry about them, and he told me they were hard, and I could use them as stepping-stones to keep my shoes out of the mud. I quickly took one step and then another by sheer gravity, and to my surprise, my shoes and socks were covered with green cow poop. My mother was not happy.

Do not forget the baby

The year after my baby brother, Conrad, was born, we visited the farm to show off the new baby. As we were leaving and driving down the hill to the main road, we looked back, and grandma and grandpa were waving, but grandma was still holding the baby. Oops. Well, it happens to the best of us.

My husband and I left our firstborn in the church nursery one Sunday, and we got all the way home before we realized it. When we got back to the church, the preacher had her in the hall and was asking her the names of her parents. She told him Mama and Daddy.

What is next?

After my husband was killed in Vietnam, I did not know what I was going to do with my life. I was attending a church that was preparing for three youth camps at Big Bear Lake in California. They were needing teachers and counselors. Even though I had never done either, I volunteered to go and be a counselor for the girls. Each youth group stayed for one week, but the teachers and counselors stayed for the entire three weeks with Saturday afternoons and Sundays off. I was given a notebook with rules, policies, my expected responsibilities, and devotional material.

I stayed with the girls in their cabin, led them to all activities, church services, and meals. It was here where God gently led me into a lifetime of serving at youth camps. Those three weeks taught me so much and instilled in my heart a desire to serve him through teaching, counseling at camp, and, later, cooking at youth camps, which lasted for over fifty years.

> Trust in the Lord with all thine heart; and
> lean not unto thine own understanding. In all
> thy ways acknowledge him, and he shall direct
> thy paths. (Proverbs 3:5, 6)

I cannot let this story go without telling you what was not in the policy notebook for counselors. Every morning, a bell rang to let the campers know it was time to wake up. But all the counselors plotted together to wake the kids up with a blast on their last morning. We played Napoleon XIV's song, "They're Coming to Take Me Away, Ha-Haaa!" as loud as we could over the speakers. It still makes me laugh.

My road to salvation

Becoming a believer was not easy for me. It happened over a period of eighteen years. The beginning of my knowledge of Jesus as a personal Savior came about when I was ten years old. We were visiting my stepdad's parents' farm, and we always went to church when we visited there in Bronson, Iowa. After church one Sunday, my grandma talked to me privately about Jesus. It was the first time I had heard things like sin, forgiveness, repentance, salvation, grace, and heaven. She talked to me for a long time. I was interested, but I did not pray with her or accept him as my personal Savior.

When our family moved to Le Mars, Iowa, and later to Marcus, Iowa, we began attending church on a regular basis. I don't remember getting anything out of those services. I had fun in the youth group activities but none of the preaching or teaching stayed with me. I was married in that Methodist church, but we attended the Lutheran church in Imperial Beach, California, all of our married life, which only lasted four years because of the Vietnam War.

After his death, I continued to attend that church and was married again in the same church. My new husband was newly saved and attending a Bible church in Vista, California. My daughter and I moved to Vista after the wedding. He continued to attend the Bible church on Sunday mornings, but my daughter and I attended my church on Sunday mornings. It was an odd beginning, but we went to church with him on Sunday nights. The Sunday night services were strange to me because people would stand up and give a testimony about something, and sometimes, they would cry about it. I felt uncomfortable.

Soon, the preacher from the Bible church was sending people to my home to talk to me about leaving my church and joining their church. I was not a fan. After many visits from other people, the pastor himself came over to convince me how mistaken I was in my theology. When he started in on me, I rudely lit up a cigarette and made sure there was a lot of smoke at that table. It started with a discussion regarding infant baptism. He challenged me to find it in the

Bible. I showed him my catechism book, and he took it from me and told me to find it in the Bible. So the challenge was on, but I could not find it in the Bible. That made me curious.

The next time he came over, he told me that some churches did not believe in hell. Well, I knew he was wrong about my church. I believed in hell as described in the Bible. So the next time I went to my church, I asked the minister about hell. He told me that he believed that we live our hell on earth and there was no literal burning hell. Well, I had read it for myself in the Bible, so I no longer trusted the catechism book and wondered what else might be an error in my theology.

After those many conversations and reading the Bible for myself, I knew that preacher was right. It was not long after that I felt the conviction to become a believer. I went forward in church during an invitation, and one of the ladies came to talk to me about the scriptures. She took me to the book of Romans (those scriptures are shared below). I was overwhelmed with guilt. I knew my sins and asked forgiveness and trusted Jesus to forgive me and save me, which he most certainly did on that day, September 1, 1968, and I was baptized that night.

> If we confess our sins, he is faithful and just to forgive us our sins and to cleanse us from all unrighteousness. If we say that we have not sinned, we make him a liar and his word is not in us. (1 John 1: 9–10)

The Roman's Road to Salvation

> As it is written, there is none righteous, no, not one: There is none that understandeth, there is none that seeketh after God. They are all gone out of the way, they are together become unprofitable, there is none that doeth good, no, not one (Romans 3:10–12)

For all have sinned and come short of the glory of God. (Romans 3:23)

Wherefore, as by one-man (Adam) sin entered into the world, and death by sin: and so, death passed upon all men for that all have sinned. (Romans 5:12)

For the wages of sin is death, but the gift of God is eternal life through Jesus Christ our Lord. (Romans 6:23)

That if thou shalt confess with thy mouth the Lord Jesus, and shalt believe in thine heart that God hath raised him from the dead, thou shalt be saved. For with the heart man believeth unto righteousness; and with the mouth confession is made unto salvation. For the scripture saith, whosoever believeth on him shall not be ashamed. (Romans 10:9–10)

For whosoever shall call upon the name of the Lord shall be saved. (Romans 10:13)

The antique table, a family heirloom

As long as I can remember, I admired a beautiful hand-carved table with a marble top that my grandparents had in their home. In the middle of the table, between the four beautiful legs with claw feet, was a hand-carved freestanding deer with a full rack. My great-uncle presented this table to my grandfather's mother upon his birth in about 1876. After the death of my grandmother, my grandfather had come to live with us in Iowa, and the table became part of our home. When I graduated from high school, my grandfather presented the table to me. After I married three years out of high school, I was preparing to move to California with my husband. My mother would not allow me to take the table with me until we were settled into a home of our own. My husband died in 1966, and by 1968, I was settled again into my second home.

My parents were coming out to visit us, and I asked my mother to bring the table with her. She refused. This time, she told me I could never have that table because it should have been given to her or one of my grandfather's sons. So, for another twenty years, the family heirloom was tucked away in a closet at my mother's house. Then in the 1990s, my little sister, Beverly, and her son were going to visit my oldest daughter in Iowa at the same time I was visiting her. She told me she was bringing me my table. It was placed in the back seat of her car.

Our mother was in a nursing home by this time, and I do not think she ever knew what my little sister did. I transported it to my home in Washington at the end of my vacation, and it has been with me ever since.

TRAVEL EXPERIENCES

All my travel experiences outside the United States are covered in my first book, *Read My Life and Travel Experiences and I will Throw in a Cake*. The following stories are the places I have traveled within the United States.

I was about seven years old when I took my first train ride. My mother and my brother and I took the train from California to Washington to visit my uncle Harry. The train was separated into three sections. There was a viewing section much like a living room with big windows and comfortable chairs. We slept in little cubbies that we entered by a set of stairs, and there was a heavy curtain that we pulled together to keep out the lights and noise. The eating section was my favorite. The table was covered with a white linen tablecloth and matching linen napkins were at each place setting along with the silverware. A waiter came to the table dressed in black slacks and a white jacket and took our order and then delivered it to us. That was the most exciting breakfast and dinner I ever experienced as a child, except for the one at the Grand Canyon.

The Grand Canyon

Our family took a vacation by car to the Grand Canyon when I was eight. It was hot, and our cooling system was on the outside of the car. It was referred to as a swamp cooler. It was on my mother's side of the car, and my brother and I took turns sitting where we could get most of the cool air. I do not remember much of the canyon, except that we viewed it from a conservatory of some sort. I do remember the restaurant because it was so unique. When you got into line to be served, you chose your main course from one of the two large metal barrels (stainless steel), which were held by chains and could be moved from front to back. When you made your choice, the waiter turned the barrel and dipped out your portion into a metal divided plate.

The plate was set on a narrow counter that ran the length of the serving area, and a waiter would add to your plate whatever else you wanted. The tables were made from logs as were the benches. There was a huge stuffed bear in one corner that must have been the pride of some taxidermist as well as deer heads all along the wall. It was very rustic, and from a child's perspective, almost scary.

My husband and I stopped to see the Grand Canyon on our way to California after our wedding thirteen years later, and I searched and asked everyone if they knew where that restaurant was, and nobody could tell me. So it became a vivid memory lost to the past.

Yabba-dabba-doo

I took many road trips with my children throughout their lives from California, Oregon, or Washington to Iowa. We stopped along the way at many tourist traps, but it was fun. One year, I took my oldest daughter, my husband's two daughters, and their half-sister, and my young son on one of those road trips. One of our main stops was at Bedrock City, the home of Fred and Wilma Flintstone. Everything there looked exactly like the scenes in the television set. I could hardly contain my son. He was everywhere at once, which was normal but still hard to control in all his excitement. The girls and I were headed to a gift shop, and after we were inside a few minutes, we realized that Matthew was not with us. So out the door we went, divided up and looked and looked. We could not find him. We went back to the gift shop to get some help when we heard that the Flintstone movies were being shown in the theater. Sure enough, there he was, happy as a clam, sitting in the front row, watching the movies. When it was time for us to get back on the road, he cried all the way to the car because we had to leave. Such drama for a little boy.

Yellowstone National Park

During that same trip, we stopped, and I rented one of the small log cabins built for the tourist spending the night in order to see Old Faithful. They were furnished with only beds and one table. It was just for one night, and I thought it would be fun for the kids. Well, it was not fun for the kids because they could see through the logs of the cabin, and it scared them. They heard strange noises outside, and there was no bathroom. I had four girls under the age of ten and one small boy afraid of the dark. Did they all need to make a trip to the camp bathroom at the same time? Of course not!

On one trip to the outhouse, a deer or something like a deer passed our path. That was a little unnerving. That being said, it was not fun for me either. However, seeing Old Faithful and the Paint Pots that smelled like sulfur was fun, and then we were on the road again.

Rapid City and Mitchell, South Dakota

I should have known better than to stop at the Reptile Gardens just outside of Rapid City. I hate snakes! It was advertised like it was a zoo as well, so we stopped for a few hours. There were a lot of other animals to see, but there were so many snakes it made me nauseous. My young son did not like the snakes either, and he clung on to my leg and, sometimes, I carried him on my back. The girls were fine, and they even participated in the touching of the snakes. Nope, not me. Not ever! The kids chose a souvenir, but they were not allowed to make their choice a snake of any kind.

After the Reptile Gardens, the Corn Palace in Mitchell was really fun. It was full of Native American exhibits, murals made from thousands of pieces of corn, husks, and various other plants that are harvested in the Midwest. We spent a lot of time there going through the exhibits and purchasing just the right souvenir. We also kept a close eye on little man who was wanting to go in all directions at the same time. I should have named him Zoom!

The kidnapping

I unknowingly participated in a kidnapping before all those road trips. My husband had the two daughters when we married, and custody was split between the two parents. Their relationship with each other was volatile. We decided to take a vacation one summer from California to Oregon for a week or so to visit his parents. His girls came on a Friday night, and we left on Saturday. He did not tell the girls or their mother that we were leaving the state. His intention was to take the girls to another state without their mother knowing they were gone until she came to pick them up after a week. He told me not to tell them either because he wanted the trip to be a surprise.

After the first week we were in Oregon, he was then bragging to his brother about his little stunt that made their mother panic. When I found out what he was doing, I called her and told her where her girls were. She showed up with the sheriff and retrieved her children. That was my first clue into his true nature. It turned out that he was cold, callous, and controlling.

Shortly after that, he took a teaching job in Vietnam and came home every six months for two weeks. The whole story of his plot to get rid of me and how it backfired is in my first book, *Read My Life and Travel Experiences and I will Throw in a Cake.*

Idleyld Park Hot Springs

I took my two youngest daughters, about fifteen and six, on a road trip to Oregon to visit their aunt and grandparents. They lived in the Idleyld Park area in the woods, close to a river. Their grandfather taught them to fish on the river. On one of the days, we decided to take a hike to the hot springs. It was a beautiful sunny day for about a two-mile hike through the woods. Someone had built a wooden gazebo over the hot springs with seating areas so you could dangle your feet or it was shallow enough for you to cover your entire body in the hot mineral water.

As we were approaching the springs, we heard voices and realized there were people there. We all walked up close enough to speak with them, and they decided they had been there for some time and would leave so we could enjoy it. We were grateful and appreciative as the people sitting on the edge were getting ready to depart. However, the young men and women that were actually in the water were completely naked and unashamed to get out before us.

Mount Rushmore

This is a wonderful place to visit. I have been four times, and each time, it is breathtaking. The sculpture began in 1927 and opened to the public in 1941. It is hard to fathom how this was even possible. The four icons carved into the mountain are George Washington, Thomas Jefferson, Theodore Roosevelt, and Abraham Lincoln. Why did the sculpturer, Gutzon Borglum, select these four men? I had no idea. So I decided to find out. They were chosen because he thought they represented the most notable events in history. Wow! Time for a little history lesson.

George Washington was the first President of the United States. He won the war on independence from Great Britain and laid the foundation of American democracy.

Thomas Jefferson was the main writer of the Declaration of Independence and purchased the Louisiana Territory from France in 1803.

Theodore Roosevelt was the twenty-sixth President of the United States when America experienced tremendous economic growth leading into the twentieth century. He was also instrumental in negotiating the building of the Panama Canal.

Abraham Lincoln was the sixteenth President of the United States and kept the nation together during the Civil War and assisted in the abolishing of slavery.

Cooking for the family on a houseboat

This was quite the adventure. My youngest daughter's husband and his family invited me to join them, and I volunteered to cook. There were eight of us on Lake Roosevelt for a week in a lovely houseboat. We each had our own private sleeping area, and there was a common kitchen and living area. The young ones brought their canoes and did a lot of swimming and floating. The older ones played dominoes and cards or just enjoyed the quiet of the river. There was a hot tub on the top deck, and the night stars were brighter than any I had ever seen.

God created the lights in the heavens, and Jesus became the Light of the world.

> Then spake Jesus again unto them, saying,
> I am the light of the world: he that followeth me
> shall not walk in darkness, but shall have the light
> of life. (John 8:12)

Tillicum Village

This was an all-day excursion with a group of friends from my church in Spokane. It began quite early in the morning with donuts and coffee as we were bused to a Seattle pier, about a three-hour ride, and then we boarded a luxurious ferry to Blake Island in Puget Sound. As soon as we arrived, we were lined up to receive a cup full of hot clams in the shell. I took the cup, but it took me a while before I decided to try to eat the slimy substance within. Actually, it was exceptionally good, which surprised me. After the clams were eaten, we were to crush the shells on the ground, which was covered with crushed shells.

Then we were ushered into the Trimble mansion, which had been restored to house a museum of interesting artifacts, a fabulous gift shop, and a large serve yourself restaurant. Our table was in front of the stage for a good close-up of the Native American storytelling program. Our salmon lunch was incredible.

Fairbanks, Alaska—a mission trip

Three of my friends from church and I decided to volunteer to cook for our mission crew that was headed to Alaska to help with a summer vacation Bible school program for one of our churches there. The mission crew was going to help with the teaching, games, and music. Our only responsibility was to cook for our group of ten. We met together and developed a menu for the eight days we would be there. We knew we would be able to purchase groceries at a Costco and a Walmart, so we also put together a grocery list. Both churches had budgeted for the food. The message was that we would be cooking in the kitchen of the four-bedroom house we would be staying in. Sounds organized, clear, and thought out, right?

Wrong!

When we arrived, we knew, first of all, we needed to shop for the groceries. We had dinner to prepare for the first evening, so off we went. We came back, put a roast in the Crock-Pot, and began to put our groceries in order. Our pastor came in to tell us that the crew organizing the VBS wanted a meeting with us. The new message was that not only would we be cooking for our crew but also for their church crew of about fifteen. Seems there was a little mix-up in communications. Added to that, we were also going to be responsible for preparing snacks for between eighty and one hundred children. Oh, and also their lunches each day. It seems the church was also a school. What!

Initially, the four of us panicked! Then we revised our menus and the rest of our grocery lists and back to the stores we went. The church gave us their credit card for the groceries, and guess what? It did not work. Our church had budgeted to help with the food, so we used our card to the max. Back at the house, putting everything away, and preparing for dinner, we discovered that there were no dishes, utensils, cookware, mixing bowls, skillets, or pans.

We decided to brew a pot of coffee and make a list of kitchen supplies. Nope, no coffee pot. One of the men left immediately for Walmart, came back with a new pot, got it ready to brew, and it would not work. Back to Walmart for another. The four of us left for our third trip to the store to furnish the kitchen so we could cook. We used our own money for this trip.

Also, that same day before all the trips to the store, we were told that three of us would not be staying in the house. We would be sharing an apartment two blocks away from the house we would be cooking in. When we unpacked at the apartment, there was one regular bed and two mattresses on the floor. There was one unkept bathroom and no toilet paper, soap, or towels, and the sink was clogged, so we purchased what was necessary for us to live in the apartment with our own money.

We went to Costco or Walmart every day we were there to provide the lunches and snacks for all those kids plus the meals for the crews. It was 105 degrees one of the days, and there were no fans or air-conditioning. It became clear to us through our new circumstances that we needed to do whatever was necessary for God's glory, not our own. Needless to say, we were exhausted when we got home, but we all knew we would do it again.

> Whether therefore ye eat, or drink, or whatsoever ye do, do all to the glory of God. (1 Corinthians 10:31)

Noah's Ark reconstructed in Kentucky

I flew to Indiana to visit my youngest daughter and her husband for a week. I asked for a special side trip to see the ark in

Williamstown, Kentucky. When we arrived in the parking lot and paid, a shuttle picked us up and took us to the top of the hill. When the ark came into view, it was utterly spectacular. It took us hours to travel through the three levels. Through modern science and technology, it suggested how the family of eight lived productive lives and how the animals were fed, watered, and cleaned up after. We were able to see the possible ways the animals were housed; the food was stored, and breakables did not get broken during the year at sea. I stood by a replica of the huge door, which the animals would have entered and exited. This amazing experience cannot be covered in this book, but I am giving you an opportunity to buy a copy of the book I bought, which explains answers to your questions regarding this miraculous voyage. For your copy, write: Master Books, PO Box 726, Green Forest, AR 72638. The book title is *Inside Noah's Ark: Why It Worked*, edited by Tim Chaffey and Laura Welch.

There were some live animals aboard the ark, cute little piglets. Outside the ark, there was a park with many diverse kinds of animals we could view and pet. There were camels there as well, and I rode one. Yep, quite the experience.

The Wizarding World of Harry Potter

My son-in-law's mother and I took a trip from Washington to Florida to visit her mother. While we were there, we spent a full day visiting Universal Studios in Orlando. We waited in line for an hour to visit the Hogwarts Castle. Hogsmeade was just like the movie set, and we had lunch and butterbeer (a sweet foamy drink that was not made with butter or beer). We took flight on the ride of the Hippogriff and nearly lost our lunch. Before the ride, they assigned each of us a locker to store everything we had with us. Nothing was allowed on the ride but yourself, and when it took off, I was fully aware of why. When we recovered, a stroll down Diagon Alley provided us with candy from Honeydukes and a stuffed owl souvenir called Hedwig.

One of my upstairs bedrooms is completely furnished with everything Harry Potter. The bed and canopy are like the boy's dorm at Hogwarts. Beside the bed lay Harry's glasses, a string of keys, and on the floor, his slippers. Hanging on a hook is Harry's Gryffindor scarf. Hedwig hangs in an old cage. I created an owlery on the window ledge. Snape has his stash of wizard's potions in a cupboard on the wall. On a table in the corner is a complete village including the replicas of the cast and the magic car. The grandkids love it.

The Titanic

While in Orlando, we visited the Titanic Museum. As we entered, we were each given a card with the name of a person who was aboard the ship. We followed the tour guide and learned about the people on our cards. Much of the tour area looked exactly like the movie set. It was remarkably interesting. The pictures and arti-facts were excellent exhibits. If you ever venture to Florida, I highly recommend that you visit here.

The Holy Land experience of Orlando

This was a Bible-based fourteen-acre theme park that depicted first-century Jerusalem. The living biblical museum took the tourist through the creation of the Bible from the manuscripts of papyrus to the completion of the King James Bible. The park opened in 2001 and closed for good in 2020. I'm glad to have the memories and pic-tures from that experience.

KIDS

> Lo, children are an heritage of the Lord:
> and the fruit of the womb is his reward. (Psalm
> 127:3)

When my kids disobeyed me, I would often ask them when they were young if they were smarter than air and water. They would look at me funny in the beginning, but then the older they got, they understood. I would recite this verse to them and remind them how important it was to obey.

> What manner of man is this, that even the
> winds and the sea obey him! (Matthew 8:27)

I wanted my kids to learn to obey at an early age so they would have no trouble obeying Jesus throughout their lives.

If you want to enjoy your grandkids, your own kids must survive your parenting and the growing up process. I have not been the perfect parent with remarkable parenting skills, and kids are ingenious when it comes to doing things that make you just shake your head. Here are some of the stories that made me shake my head and/or laugh aloud.

Daughter, about 7: The doctor told me that she needed her tonsils out. I took her to the hospital the day before her surgery. She was in a room with another little girl that was having the same surgery. They became fast friends and were laughing and playing around. One of her favorite snacks was gingerbread, so I told her I would bring it to her that evening.

I brought the gingerbread on cute plates with whipped cream on top and sprinkles for both girls. I also brought books, games, and stuffed animals for each of them. It did not take long for them to be in party mode. My daughter was having so much fun, giving me hugs, and telling me thank you. Finally, it was time for me to leave.

The surgery was scheduled for 7:00 a.m. I arrived at the hospital about 8:00 a.m. When I entered her room, she was so mad, she would not even look at me. I tried to hug her and talk with her, and she would have none of it. I took her home and gave her all the popsicles she wanted, but she would not speak to me. That attitude lasted for about five days. I had to go into my room and shut the door to laugh my head off. I dared not for her see me laugh.

> And ye fathers (this means mothers, too)
> provoke not your children to wrath. (Ephesians
> 6:4)

While my children were young, my discipline was to spank only when they deliberately disobeyed. They only got two to three swats as they were bending over their bed with their hands above their heads.

> He that spareth his rod hateth his son:
> but he that loveth him chasteneth him betimes.
> (Proverbs 13:24)

Son and stepson, about 8 and 6: I do not remember what the boys did to deserve their swats, but they went to their room to get into position. I tried always to wait until I could go in and administer the discipline without being angry or laughing. When I entered their room, both boys were on their knees with their hands over their heads. The first swat sounded a little out of the ordinary. The second swat gave me pause to ask them what they had in their pants. They confessed and both pulled out two of their Golden Books from the back of their jeans. Discipline over!

Stepson, about 7: I remember this offense. He was dressed for church and asked if he could wait outside. I let him go out, but I specifically told him to stay away from the puddle of oil in the carport. He did not. He had oil on his shoes and on the legs of his trousers.

I sent him to his room to get into position. Minutes later, he came down the hall crying and told me he did not want a spanking, so could I just ground him? I said no, and he returned to his room. Minutes after that, he came down the hall again, crying, and told me he did not want a spanking, so could he just work it off? I said no, and he returned to his room. Once again, down the hall, crying, and told me he did not want a spanking, so could I just talk to him? I just wanted to give it up at that point because I was having a tough time being serious, but he got his two swats and a change of clothes.

> Children, obey your parents in all things:
> for this is well pleasing unto the Lord. (Colossians
> 3:20)

Son, about 11: The boys played in the woods behind our house and, one day, I went to the woods because I felt like I needed to check on them. When I reached their play area, my son was up in a tree. His friends had dragged an old beat-up mattress from somewhere (who knows?) and had put it under the tree my son was sitting in. He was crouching like he was about to jump out of that tree, onto that mattress. I stopped that process at once! However, just recently, he confessed to me (age fifty-four) that he and his friends had jumped out of that tree on numerous occasions and onto whatever they had dragged from the dump. I am glad God has angels to watch over our children when we cannot.

Stepson, about 10: Saturdays should be sacred for parents. We just want to sleep in a little bit longer, rise from our beds slowly, and enjoy a quiet cup of coffee before the chaos of the weekend begins. But no, we had to take a drastic measure to get this one little boy to be quiet on Saturday mornings.

After he was sound asleep on Friday night, we made a large sign that read "IF WE HEAR ONE SOUND OUT OF YOU, YOU WILL BE GROUNDED FOR LIFE." We taped that sign on the inside of his door. But that is not all. We also taped newspapers across the doorway from top to bottom so if he opened his door, he was unable to leave his room without breaking through the newspapers and making a lot of noise. It worked.

Son, about 12: He was happily licking on a giant jawbreaker. Then he said, "Watch this, Mom." He threw it up in the air with the intent of catching it in his gaping mouth. It landed in his mouth, all right, but not before breaking a front tooth. This was one of those moments when you just shake your head and head for the dentist.

Daughter, about 4: I bought her an Easy-Bake Oven, and she liked to play with it in the living room where the family spent time together. I had to plug it into an extension cord so it could be where she wanted it. When she finished playing, she tried to unplug it from the extension cord, but she could not do it. So she leaned over and tried to pull the plug out with her teeth. Well, the sparks flew, and she screamed. It scared me too. I called the hospital and spoke with a nurse. She thought she would be all right but suggested a doctor should look at her. It turned out that she was okay, but it burned her lip, and she still has a scar on the inside of her lip. It is scary being a parent sometimes.

Daughter, about 4: She received a Baby Alive doll for Christmas, and she had a little high chair for it. Her doll came with a packet of special food that you mixed with water. She could feed her doll with a spoon and later change her diaper just like Mommy did with her baby. One evening, she fed her doll the food and waited for it to end up in her little diaper. She laid her doll down to change her diaper and did the funniest thing that made us all roar with laughter and gag a little at the same time. She used her little spoon to scoop up what was in the doll's diaper and shoved it right back into her doll's mouth. Ugh!

Son, about 3: I always liked to sit toward the front in church so I would not be distracted by talkers or unruly children. I took notes and wanted to hear everything as well. This morning, sitting about four rows from the front, I was sitting with my two children. I needed to leave the pew for a few minutes, and I left my purse behind. My friend told me later that she cleared two rows of pews to tackle my son. He had rummaged through my purse and found a single wrapped feminine necessity, stood up in the pew with it between his fingers, and acted like he was smoking a cigar.

Son, about 4: He developed a good-sized hernia and spent a day in the hospital after the surgery. The doctor released him but cautioned me to limit his activities and to keep him calm and quiet indoors for a couple of days. Sounds easy enough. I barely got our van parked in the driveway before he had opened the sliding door, jumped out, ran for the house and straight into the backyard. When I reached the backyard, he was chasing the dog and whooping it up. My thoughts were, *Oh well, whatever will be will be.*

Son, about 4: No seat belts back then, and he always stood up in the front seat while I was driving with his arm around my neck. We were almost home when he told me he had to go potty. I told him we would be home in just a few minutes. Then I quickly forgot and stopped at a little convenience store for milk. I told him to wait in the car, which he usually did playing with the steering wheel. I ran in and right back out, only to find him standing on the seat with the door open, relieving himself on the car next to us.

Daughter, about 8, and cousin: The kids were staying a few days with my dad and stepmom on their ranch in Myrtle Point, Oregon. They usually had a lot of fun and rarely got into any trouble. However, one afternoon, the girls were playing in the backyard where Charlene had planted her favorite flowers, bright orange bottlebrush. There was a full garden of these beautiful flowers in full bloom. The girls cut the blooms off every flower in the garden. Why? I have no idea, and neither do they! Their punishment was light. My stepmom only had two types of punishment. The kids would have a choice to either do the dishes or clean out the goat barn. My dad's punishment was to either stack wood or clean out the goat barn.

Daughter, a toddler: All by herself, she broke off every branch she could reach of my beautiful hardy Jerusalem ivy plant hanging from the ceiling in a plant holder. I had nurtured that plant for years because it was the only plant that had ever lived through my care. When I found her, she was sitting among the broken leaves and branches, smiling and incredibly happy with herself. What can you do? Just shake your head and move on.

Daughter, about 7: I took a road trip with my youngest daughter from Oregon to Sacramento to visit my oldest daughter. While we were there, we went to the Sacramento County Fair. One of the attractions was a live rock band, so we sat down to listen. They played and they danced to some of their music. Before they ended their program, they invited anyone in the audience to come up and dance with them. My seven-year-old jumped out of her seat and ran to the stage. She danced with them and tried to copy all their moves. The leader of the band was cheering her on, and she was having a blast. She is a good dancer to this day.

Son, about 4: During bath time, I usually let them have toys in the tub and limited the amount of water. This way, I felt like I could leave them safely playing and do other things. He had his cars and trucks to begin with but got out of the tub and gathered three of his sister's dolls, unbeknownst to me. Then I heard some remarkably familiar language coming from the bathroom. It sounded like this, "I baptize you in the name of the Father, Son, and Holy Ghost. Buried in the likeness of his death and raised again to newness of life." I sneaked to the door as he was baptizing those dolls and repeating the same words used at a real baptism.

Son, about 6: During his year in kindergarten, his teacher was preparing a program for the parents. She was going to ask her students what they wanted to be when they grew up. My son was excited to tell her that he wanted to be a preacher. Every time we asked him, he said the same thing, he wanted to be a preacher. The night of the program came, and we were the proud parents of a kid who wanted to be a preacher. When it was his turn, the teacher asked him what he wanted to be when he grew up, and he replied, "I want to be a garbage truck driver."

Pupkits?

We were getting ready to move into a new house with lots of yard and room for pets. The kids were young, and some were asking for a puppy, and some wanted kittens. I was being funny and told them that after we moved, we would raise "pupkits," which I told them were part puppy and part kitten. They thought that was the greatest thing they had ever heard. However, it came later to bite me because I did not clarify with them that I was just joking. The youngest went to school and told the class that we were going to raise "pupkits" in our new backyard. The teacher sent home a note admonishing me. I had to explain to the kiddos that I was only joking. From then on, I made sure my children knew when I was joking around with them.

Son, about 6: I had a nine-passenger van, and sometimes, I would pick up other children for Sunday school. One morning, both of my children were in the very back of the van. I got in, and there was a pile of oily rags on the seat beside me. I did not know how or why they were there, but they did not smell good, so I reached over to throw them out my window. As I touched them, something moved, and as I lifted the rags, a huge horny toad made his move for me. I screamed, and within an instant, my son cleared the middle seats and was out of the van and standing on the front porch.

I leaped out on my side and, immediately, the neighbor came out to see what the matter was. He gentlemanly removed the toad, but he had a smile on his face. Two of the teen boys from the youth group drove right by my house as they were picking up children and dropped off the horny toad to my van.

Son, about 13: We bought him a BB gun for Christmas and set up a firing range in the backyard. We gave him two specific rules: one, do not point your BB gun at people or animals; and two, do not shoot your BB gun in the house. Simple enough, right? After the holidays, I decided to rearrange the living room (a woman's prerogative, you know). I began with the furniture and then the wall decor.

As I was taking down the pictures and plaques and dusting them, I began to notice little holes all over the wooden plaques. Yep, BB holes. I followed the path of the little holes and concluded that he positioned himself on the couch and shot several holes in each of the wooden plaques on the surrounding walls. There were not that many, but the ones that were there were plaques he and his siblings had made out of wood and decoupaged for me. One I really cherished was a picture of him in his Civil Air Patrol uniform flanked by the American flag and the Constitution. Well, I could say, now it was holey, but I did not. He confessed, but you know, as parents, they only confess when they are caught and the evidence is overwhelming.

West Coast Game Park Safari

This was a wonderfully fun experience for me and for all my children at different ages in their lives. It was only a couple of hours from where we lived and an all-day adventure. My favorite were the tiger cubs we could pet and watch play. We had to stay alert though. I let the little man who wanted to be everywhere all at once travel around by himself. However, he must have frightened a turkey wandering around because that turkey went after him. He was a little traumatized, but even that did not slow him down.

Son and stepson, about 15 and 13: They were eating all the time, and they ate a lot. One evening, I served spaghetti, salad, and French bread. They heaped up their plates to the absolute maximum with the spaghetti. When dinner was finished, it was their turn to do the dishes, so they were on it. About an hour later, when the dishes were done, they asked if they could have a peanut butter sandwich. They felt like they had worked off their dinner. They each built a peanut butter and jelly sandwich using four slices of bread each and three layers of peanut butter and jelly. That was their normal peanut butter and jelly sandwich, always. There are eighteen slices of bread in a loaf, not including the two heels, which of course the kids would not eat. When all of them wanted a sandwich for lunch, the boys used up eight slices, and each of the girls used two slices each, so there goes a loaf of bread. Often, to finish off the whole loaf, they had a friend or two over for lunch as well.

Son and stepson, about 14 and 12: Our house was at the top of a hill, which sloped down about five blocks before it reached an intersection with a mini mall on the corner. The boys took off on one bike with my stepson hanging on for dear life behind my son. They were absolutely fearless. They made it down the hill without incidence, but when they rounded into the parking lot of the mall, my stepson's leg came into direct contact with a fire hydrant. He fell off the bike in pain, and I was called. I took him to the emergency room. About six inches of his shinbone was exposed and full of gravel. He would not let go of my hand while the doctor was cleaning it up. However, the doctor had the nurse escort me out of room, fearful that I was about to faint. He was right, and I was out of there. I am definitely not nurse material.

Son, about 14: Somehow, my son came into possession of a skateboard. I cannot imagine that I would have purchased it for him considering his fearlessness. I do know that when riding a skateboard, your body is to be in a standing position, and you use one leg to propel you forward. Not my son. He was in a prone position on top of the skateboard when he took off down the same hill in front of our house. Well, he crashed to a stop and came home with open wounds from his chin down and both hands. Because of these kinds of behavior, I always told him he would never make to the age of fifteen.

When I look back at his life now, over the last fifty years, I realized that he escaped death many times as a child, a teen, in the military, and as a firefighter. He has a book of his own to write. Now he enjoys retirement by helping the homeless, taking care of veterans, serving in his church, and teaching the Bible whenever he can. I am proud of him. He probably had way more than two guardian angels watching over him.

Son, about 5: We had just moved from sunny California where all the kids had loved to go to the beach. It was always warm and sunny there. In Oregon, it was colder than what we were used to. The first trip we took to the beach was sad. We were all walking in the chilly dunes close to North Bend, Oregon, when my son saw the ocean. His shoes were already off, and he began to run for the water, slinging his jacket, shirt, and trousers off as he went. He ran into the ocean waves and came straight up out of the water, crying. He was so upset because the water was so cold. Visiting the beaches in Oregon only happened a few times during the summers, and the kids played in the tidepools rather than directly in the ocean.

Daughter, about 14: She was the last one at home, and we each had our own cat. My cat was an indoor cat named Rosie. Her cat was an outdoor cat named Maggie. Rosie was old, and she had been a stray. I fed her and, one day, she came into the house and would never go out again. Maggie, on the other hand, went out into the world and gave me three funny stories to share.

My daughter got her when she was barely weaned from her mother. She was fluffy and soft, but when she was wet, she looked emaciated although she was completely healthy. When she came into heat for the first time, we did not let her go outside. She cried, howled, and paced to get out for several days and nights until my daughter and I were exhausted.

Finally, one evening, we could not stand it anymore, so we put her into my car in the driveway for the night and got a peaceful night of sleep. The next morning, as my daughter went out to retrieve her cat from the car, she called for me to look outside. There were five or six cats circling the car, one on the roof and one on the hood, looking in. It was hilarious!

She brought Maggie in, and I called the vet. I told her we needed to bring Maggie in to be spayed. She told me they would not spay her while she was in heat. I told her if that were the case, then I wanted drugs. "Oh no," she said, "we will not give her drugs."

I told her I was joking, that I would be the one needing drugs if we had to wait. Then the vet decided she would go ahead to take her in.

We lived close to the apple orchards and, occasionally, we would see a little fruit bat. They are small and brown. Maggie came into the house, one day, dragging something almost as big as she was. She was not wanting us to bother her as she dragged it into the living room. It was a large black bat still alive in her teeth and claws. It scared us both when she let go of the bat. My daughter was yelling, "Kill it, Mom."

I went for the broom, but I did not have the heart to kill it. I found a box with a lid and finally covered the bat with the box and slid the lid under. I told my daughter to open the back door, and I ran for it with the bat in the box. When I got to the door, I threw the whole box out the door as hard as I could. The box fell to the ground, and the bat flew off.

My son-in-law came to the house often but was not a fan of cats. One evening, he commented to us that he was full of gas, and we all told him to go outside. On his way out, he stopped in front of Maggie who was sitting in a chair, turned his back on her face, and expelled a good amount of that gas. Maggie gagged and sneezed about three times.

Son, about 12: "Look, Mom, I have hair on my chest!"

I would tell him I did not see any hair on his chest.

"You have to look sideways!"

So I would look at his chest from the side and comment on the five hairs. Boys are always wanting to grow up fast and become men.

Son, about 10: I was saying prayers with my son at bedtime, and he prayed that the Lord would hurry up and make his legs grow long enough to reach the gas pedal so he could drive.

Daughter, about 15: I was teaching her how to drive a stick shift because her grandfather was giving her his used Volkswagen Beetle. My son was in the back seat, wanting to be in on the action, and we took off for the school parking lot. She could not get synchronized between the clutch and the gas pedal, so we sort of jumped along the road. My son was being thrown around the back seat to the point that he jumped out of the car while it was still moving and walked home.

GRANDKIDS

My son gave me my first grandchild. His name is Jordan. He was born with a hole in his heart, and he only lived for twenty minutes. It was devastating to the entire family. I will never forget the doctor walking down the hospital corridor with Jordan cuddled on his shoulder. However, we were encouraged by the biblical words of David after the death of his first son, and I am looking forward, one day, to meeting Jordan in heaven.

> But now he is dead, wherefore should I fast?
> Can I bring him back again? I shall go to him,
> but he shall not return to me. (2 Samuel 12:23)

My first granddaughter came along a year or so later, but just before she was born, her father nearly lost his eyesight. He was cleaning out some junk from a house they were about to rent. The house was about thirty years old, and the woman who lived there all those years had several cats. Over the years, she disposed of the cat litter in one big pile near to the house. The junk from the house was laid on top of the litter pile. When all was finished, my son, who was a firefighter, poured gasoline on top of the pile and lit it on fire. It exploded like a bomb and burned the front part of his body, including his face, his eyes, and his hair. The explosion was so loud that it shattered a window at the neighbor's house.

My son was taken to the hospital, and his head and face were wrapped. He was afraid that he wouldn't be able to see his daughter at birth, but his eyes did heal, and his vision was restored. He told me later that his firefighter buddies never let him forget it, and he had to pay money into their "dumbass fund."

Granddaughter, about 6: I took the grandkids to a farm in Spokane where we could pick apples. They also housed a menagerie of farm animals that we could feed. At the end of the day, we shopped in the store, and the grandkids were looking for a souvenir. My grandkids love stuffed animals. She picked out a cute little stuffed goat with two horns on its head and asked if she could have it, and I told her yes. Then, very loudly, she announced, "I'm going to name him Horny."

The store became silent for a moment, and then we weren't the only ones laughing. I told her she should pick a new name, and she asked me why. I told her to ask her daddy. Nope, not my kid. I do not have to explain that. Grandparenting is great.

Grandson, about 2: I caught him in the bathroom, one day, standing in a big pile of toilet paper pulled from the roll. He was just standing there with his blanket and his two fingers in his mouth. I asked him, "What did you do?"

He replied, "Nothing."

I asked him, "Did you pull all this toilet paper off the roll?"

He replied, "No."

I asked, "Who did?"

He replied, "I don't know."

We were the only two people in the house.

Grandson, about 3: My daughter and I were traveling with him, and we stopped at a McDonald's restaurant that had a kids play area. He got in with all the colored plastic balls, and he was delighted. When it came time to leave, we tried to take him out, and he would not get out. His mother went in after him, and he threw the biggest loudest tantrum ever. It just made us laugh, and the more we laughed, the louder he screamed. She walked him to the car in full tantrum mode that did not let up for a long time.

Another tantrum time about the same age as we were on our way to some place he knew was going to be fun. He was in the back seat, in his car seat, all happy until we pulled up to an ATM to get some cash for the day. He thought we had arrived at an alternate destination and went into that full tantrum mode. Again, we laughed, and he screamed. How do you not laugh in these situations when they are so funny? I cannot do it!

Granddaughter, about 3: We are on our way into Walmart to do some shopping. Just inside the door is a kiddy car with the basket on top. She jumps in behind the wheel, and her older brother gets in beside her. These kiddy cars are so big and hard to push around. If it were my own kids, I would have put them in a regular basket. But with grandkids, it is hard to say no, so here we are. She pretended to drive the entire time we were in the store, even though her older brother begged for the chance to drive. Her brother was a bit too big to be seated in that car, anyway, and could barely get in and out. When it came time to leave, she refused to get out of the kiddy car. So I told her she could drive it to the basket rack in the parking lot. I was actually doing the pushing.

When we got there, she refused to get out. I emptied the basket of groceries into my van, and her brother jumped in. She refused to get out. I commenced to pull her out, and she commenced to scream. So I gave her an ultimatum. She gets out of the kiddy car and into my van or my van is going home without her. She refused to get out, so I got into my van and acted like I was leaving the parking lot. She made no move to get out, so I had to back up from my ultimatum and physically remove her from the kiddy car, even though she was screaming. Strapped into her car seat in my van, she screamed most of the way home. I lost that battle by giving her an ultimatum I could not carry out. Let that be a lesson.

Granddaughter, about 6: I took her to the petting zoo in Walters, Oregon. As we were arriving, they were bringing out a giant python for the kids to pet. As we approached, she did not even ask if she could pet it. She just ran off toward it. I called for her to come back, but she responded by telling me to come and pet it. I hate snakes, but you already know that. How can you get out of it gracefully when her little hands were all over it? I hesitated, but she grabbed my hand and put it right on that snake. Oh my gosh, I almost threw up. It was dry and smooth but an experience I do not ever want to duplicate.

Grandson, about 4: I picked him up with his two-year-old sister to spend a week with me in Spokane. They were riding in the back seat, together in their car seats. My grandson said, "I think she pooped her diaper."

I pulled over and checked, but she was dry. A few more miles down the road, and my grandson said, "Grandma, she pooped her diaper."

I pulled over at a gas station and checked, and she was dry. I asked my grandson why he keeps thinking she has pooped her diaper, and he said, "Because she stinks."

Eventually, I figured it out when I realized he was expelling gas of his own and blaming it on his sister.

Granddaughter, about 4: She and I were shopping, and she was sitting in the basket, sorting out all the groceries. All of a sudden, I heard the fire alarm and told her we needed to leave the store. I began to move toward the door, and she said to me, "Grandma, it's your phone."

Sure enough, it was my phone. I didn't recognize the sound because my son-in-law loved to change the ring tones when I wasn't looking.

Another time, I was traveling down the road, and I heard a police siren. I quickly pulled off to the side of the road. I could still hear the siren but no police car. Yep, you guessed it. It was my phone.

Grandson, about 2: I put him into the bathtub for a short bath before bed. I added several of his action figures and not much warm water. I left the bathroom, but a few minutes later, I ran in again because he was screaming. When I got to him, he was frantic and climbing out of the tub. I wrapped him in a towel, and he clung to me. What on earth? Well, there was one small brown poop floating on top of the water, and that is what scared him.

Grandson, about 5: He was visiting my house and using the bathroom. All of a sudden, he began to cry as he came out of the bathroom, saying, "I can't flush the toilet."

We asked him why, and he replied, "Because of Spiderman."

My oldest daughter followed him to the bathroom and retrieved Spiderman from the bottom of the toilet where he had just done his potty. From then on, when she wanted him to do something for her, she reminded him that with her own hand, she had reached into the toilet to save Spiderman for him.

Grandson, about 7: From an early age, my oldest grandson could recite the words from about any movie he had ever seen. My all-time favorite comes from the movie, *Despicable Me*. He could quote the following and sound just like Gru, giving the three little girls the house rules: "Rule number three, you will not cry or whine or laugh or giggle or sneeze or burp or fart or any annoying sounds."

Granddaughter, about 13: Whenever this child was in trouble, her mother made her do the dishes or the laundry. They lived on farm property in Iowa. She was given a large basket of clothes to hang on the line, but instead, she dumped them between the house and the clothesline. There were always clothes on the line, so, apparently, her mother did not notice until after a storm, when she saw her underwear and other items caught on the fence behind her house as the farmer was cultivating his beans. When given baskets of laundry to fold and put away, this same child would hide them behind the couch.

Granddaughter, about 7: She was adopted at the age of seven, and she wanted everyone to think she was seventeen. She got over that real fast. During her first day, she refused to eat the oatmeal what was served to her. Her mom let her get down from the table, but she was served the same food at the next meal. She still refused to eat it. She was allowed to leave the table, but she was again served the same food at the next meal. That day, she was served oatmeal three times and did not eat it until the next morning at breakfast. She was served oatmeal, and she ate it right down without complaint. She never again refused to eat anything that was served to her. Sometimes we do not need to be angry when they act naughty. We only need to persevere.

Granddaughter, about 12: Many girls at this age are wanting to start shaving their legs and underarms. However, this child shaved off one eyebrow. Why? She had no idea!

Warrior

Tillicum Village

Corn Palace

Kinz Rice Crispy Treats

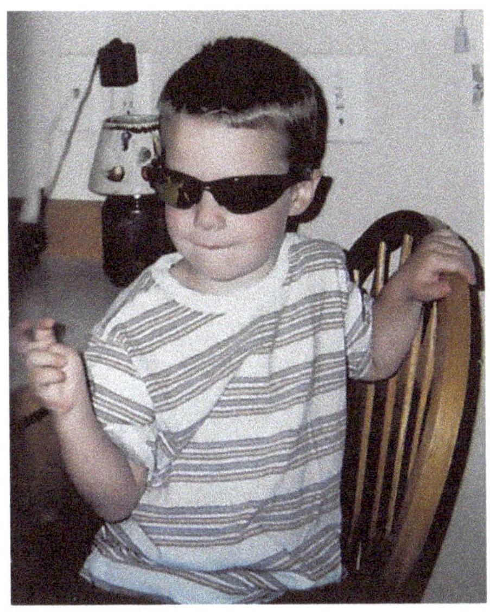

Brady's a Cool Dude

Never Too Old For Dolls

Cari's Family

Antique Table

TP'd Dad's Truck

Maddie & Kitty

His Own Tablet

Grand Canyon Deer

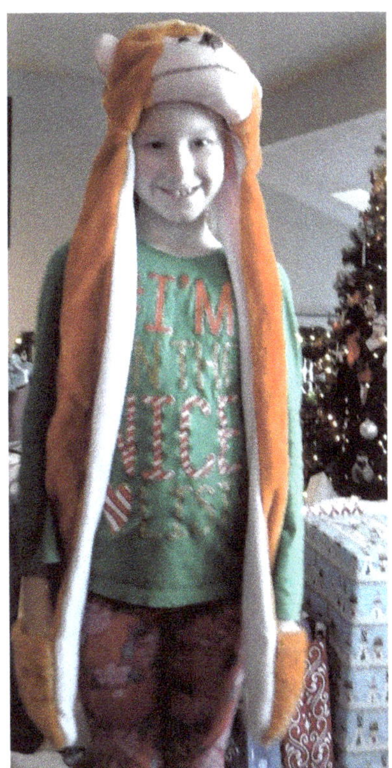

Hat with Pockets

New Bear Stuffie for G'ma

TP'd Dad's Truck

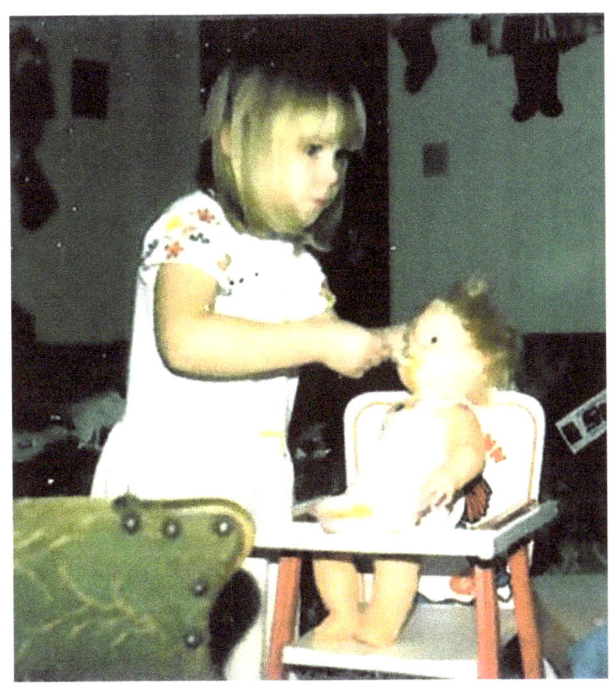

Cari & Baby Alive

Bucket Head Jett

Candy Heaven

Covered Ears for Bible Reading

Maid Marion

My Favorite Book

All My Kids at Jana's Wedding

Handsome Son, Matt

Firefighter Matt

Soldier Matt

Cari's Four

Jett With The Tongs

Two Fingers & Blankie

Just Like A Boy

Beloved Kitty Jackie Chan

Let's Eat

Can't Have Too Many Stuffies

The Lioness, Maddie

Judy at the Well

Fashion Show

Filling Dad's Shoes

Flour Roads

Hang On Grandson

Judy's Birthday

Hedwig's Mom

Oregon Hot Springs

"I didn't Do It"

All My Girls

About the Author

Judy Ann Tarvin was born in Inglewood, California. She was raised there until she was ten years old, and her family moved to the Midwest. She graduated from high school in Marcus, Iowa, married her high school sweetheart, and moved to California where her husband was stationed at Camp Pendleton with the marine corps.

After four years of marriage and one daughter, he was killed in Vietnam. She married again, attended college, and raised a son and two more daughters.

She retired after twenty-five years, working in banks and credit unions as a specialist in cardholder disputes and bank fraud. After three years of retirement, she began working again in the medical records department for Confluence Health in Wenatchee, Washington, where she continues to work.

Her hobbies include reading, writing, watching college basketball, especially Gonzaga, and being active in the Operation Christmas Child program sponsored by Samaritan's Purse. She attends Evergreen Baptist church in Cashmere and loves spending time with family and grandchildren.

www.ingramcontent.com/pod-product-compliance
Lightning Source LLC
Chambersburg PA
CBHW040158160726
48006CB00014B/1805